Leslie
in photographs

Kirkcaldy District Libraries

Leisure and Direct Services Division
Kirkcaldy District Libraries, East Fergus Place, Kirkcaldy KY1 1XT

Leslie in old photographs

Front cover pictures:
The Onoto Pen Factory
The Green, with Christ's Kirk
The Leslie bus

ISBN 1 869984 05 6

Published by
Kirkcaldy District Libraries
East Fergus Place, Kirkcaldy KY1 1XT

Printed by
Cordfall Ltd
0141 332 4640

Contents

Introduction

Leslie in photographs is the third in a series of books published by Kirkcaldy District Libraries to bring to the notice of the public the large and varied collection of photographs in our local studies collection.

We are always looking for new material. If you would like to contribute to the collection you can hand photographs in to any library. Should you not wish to part with your photo, then we would be happy to be allowed to copy it and return the original safely to you.

We are indebted to Mr. J. Muirhead and the people of Leslie who supplied information for the captions.

We hope you enjoy this collection and that it brings back many happy memories.

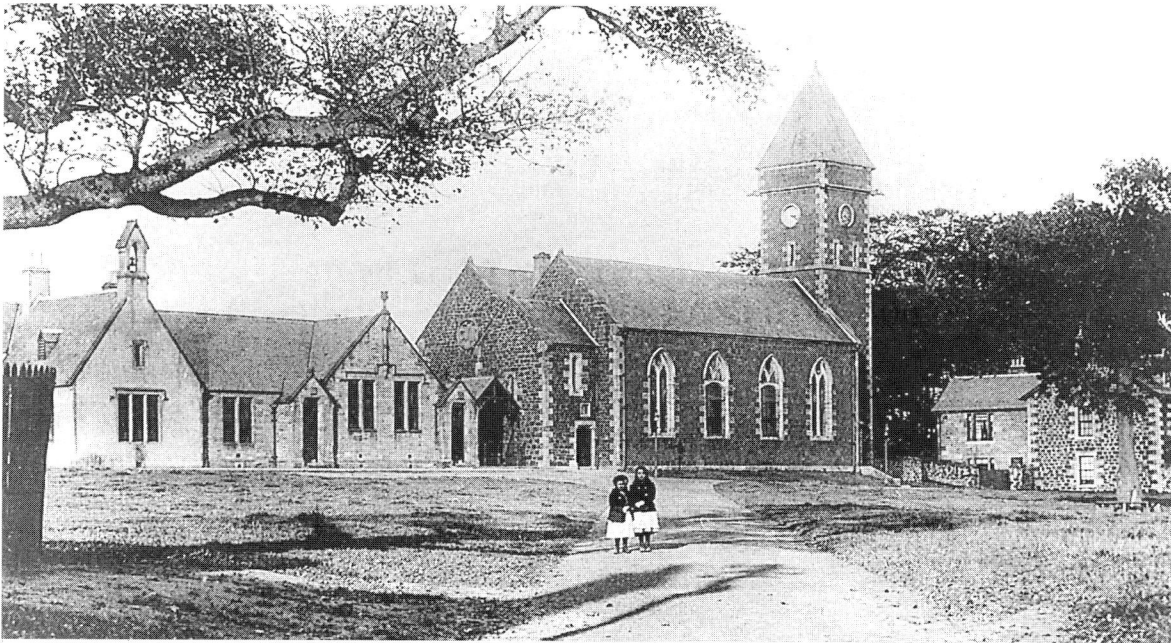

The Green, with Christ's Kirk, centre, the Manse on the right and the school on the left. The Church is being converted into flats. It was said to be the original of the poem Christ's Kirk on the Green *by James I. The school was demolished in the mid 1960s to make way for housing.*

The Dule Tree, or tree of sorrow, was the site where hangings and other punishments took place on Leslie Green. The tree became dangerous and was cut down in 1903.

Fettykil House c1902.

5

*Countess Lodge, Leslie House, 1913. It was later renamed Duchess Lodge.
In 1902 ground near the turret subsided, revealing a secret chamber.*

*Leslie House, originally known as Villa De Rothes, was built in 1667-74 in
the form of a square. It was destroyed by fire on Christmas morning, 1763.
The present house, now a Church of Scotland home for the elderly, is the
rebuilt west wing.*

Strathendry House, built by Robert Douglas of Strathendry in the early 19th century.

Leslie House, rear view.

*Above: Employees of Prinlaws Mills during the First World War who worked with flax.
The ladies wearing ties were leading hands.*

Opposite, Top: Prinlaws Mills c1900, looking over the bleachfields to the north mill.

Opposite, Bottom: Prinlaws bleachfield workers 1920s.

Below: Walkerton Mills had a troubled history. From 1891 to 1903 they were operated by William and James Livingstone. The mills reopened during the First World War, but closed shortly afterwards.

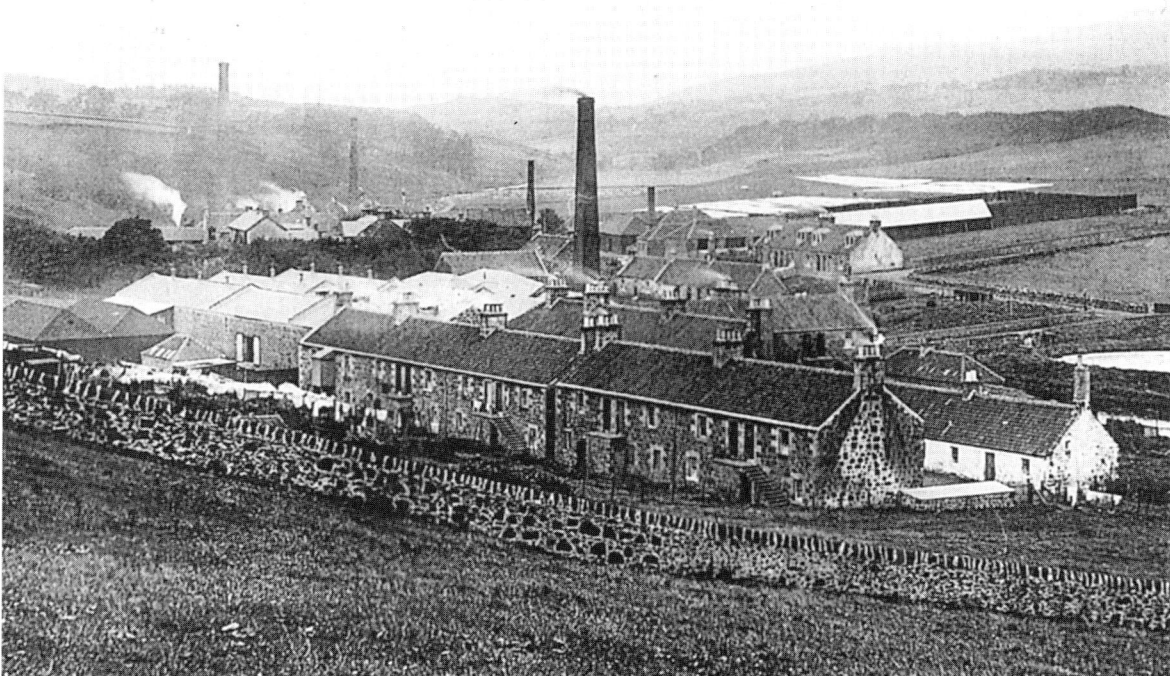

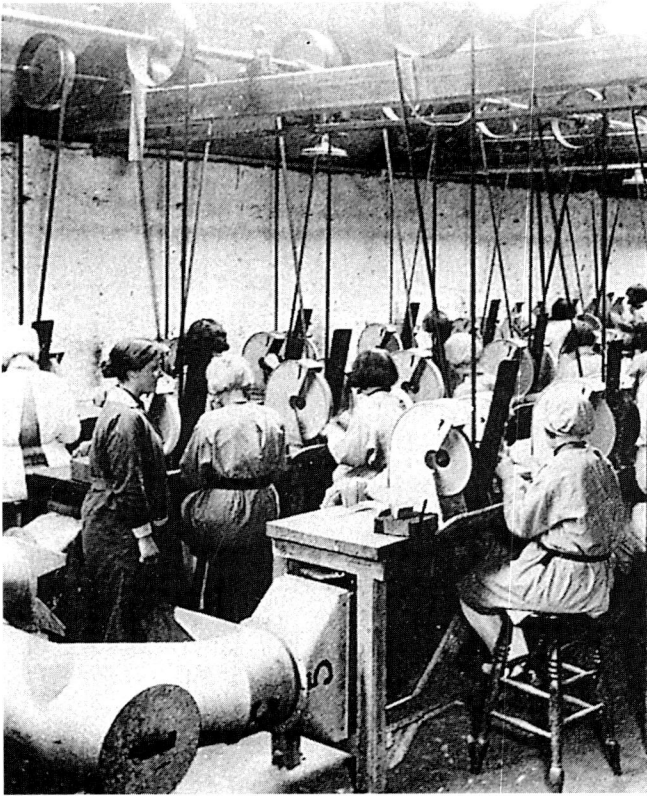

The Onoto Pen Factory: A view of the Polishing Machines.
1930s workers in the gold shop had their overalls cleaned by the firm to salvage the gold dust. During the war the company made few pens, turning instead to making aeroplane seats.

Gas works and The Croft c1908.

De La Rue's Onoto Pen Factory opened in 1927 taking over Weir and Co's paper
mill. In 1958 the firm moved to Glenrothes, where they were taken over by Intercobra.

The Onoto Pen Factory: Section of the Capstan Shop on the Manufacture of Small Parts.
In this photo, taken in the 1940s, the staff are no longer wearing uniforms because of
clothing coupon restrictions.

High Street. Turner's shop, on the left, made confectionary at Cabbagehall.

High Street, east.

Douglas Road c1920.

High Street, 1930s. Note the car in front of the petrol pump. Its registration was AFG 878.

The Cross.
These two photographs taken about 50 years
apart show little change.
The barber's shop belonged to Mr Haining.

The Cross c1952. The barber's shop is now a café with the ice cream van parked outside.

Norman Place, early 1930s,
with the Post Office on the
right.

The Leslie bus, run by Smith in the 1920s and 1930s from a garage in Ravenscraig Street, Kirkcaldy.
Competition from larger firms forced them off the road.

Fire engine at Leslie School.

The Bull Stone, Leslie Green, where bulls were tied during bull baiting. Bull baiting was abolished in 1835.

Leslie from the Viaduct c1948.

Leslie from the golf course.

Bingartree House.

Church with the steeple was known as the Logan Church, after the minister. The two churches joined after the death of Rev. Martin.
Trinity Church, on the left, was turned into a cinema but burned down in 1921. The Masonic Hall now stands on the site.

Greenside c1930, showing the War Memorial and primary school.

GREENSIDE, LESLIE   JARVIS

Braehead c1905. The church on the right is Trinity Church.

Co-op building and Y. M. C. A., with Cabbagehall on the right.

Rothes Arms Hotel, now the Greenside Hotel c1903. The hotel was part of Rothes's estate and was sold in 1919 when the estate was put on the market.

East Prinlaws 1914. The smaller houses, owned by the mill, are now listed buildings.

Rothes Arms Hotel, 1906.

Mansefield c1904.

High Street c1904 with the Post Office on the right.

Prinlaws pillars, a local landmark, marked the boundary between Leslie and Prinlaws village. The hall on the right was built as a school for older children and half-timers.

High Street c1903. The Co-op is on the left corner with Cabbagehall going off to the left.

High Street. The parade, during the First World War, was to collect money for the war effort. The nurses probably came from Leslie House which had been utilised as a hospital. The Rothes Oak Tavern is on the left.

352 Lodge Rothes was formed on 11th December, 1872. In 1884 it ceased to exist and was reconstituted on 18th April, 1908. This photograph was taken soon after it reformed.

Leslie Amateur Dramatic Society, founded in 1914, is said to be one of the oldest in Scotland. Note the footlights.

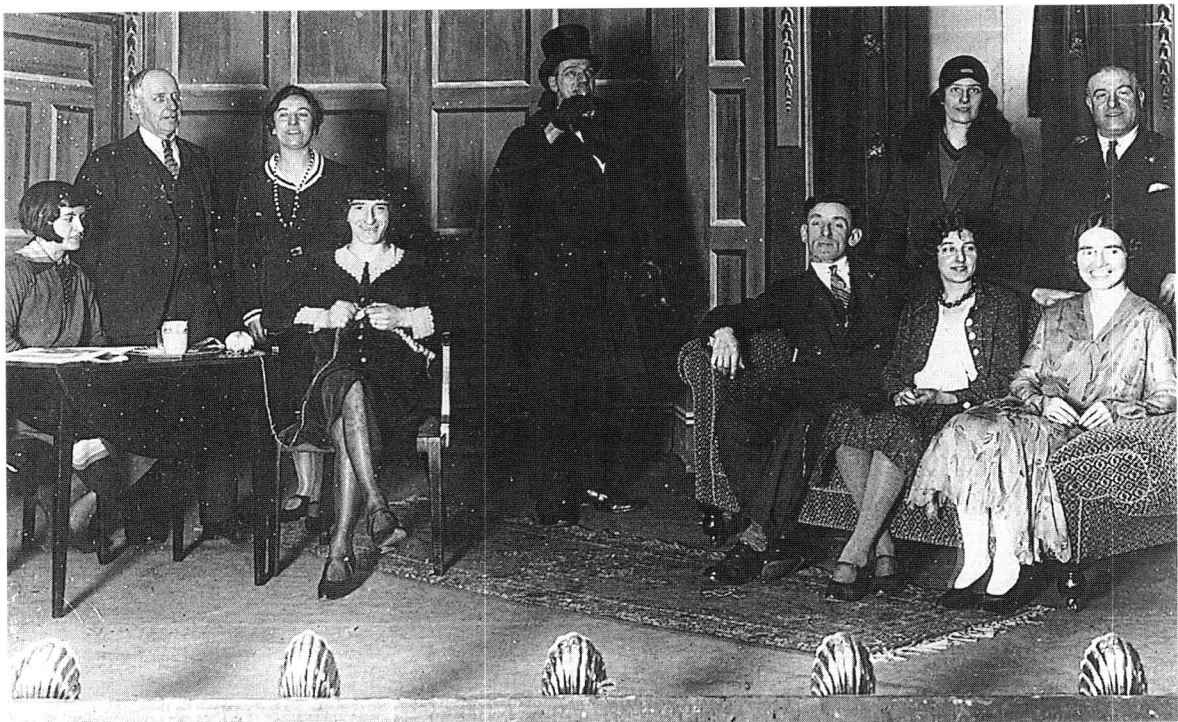

Leslie and District Silver Band 1928.
C. M. Terras, seated centre front, was the band-master for many years.

The Choral Society was founded c1928 and disbanded c1941.
This photograph dates from 1929/30.

Leslie Primary School.

Pupils enjoying the first free issue of school milk.

Staff of Leslie School in the 1920s.

Parade to the first ladies football match at Prinlaws Park between Coaltown Ladies and Tullis Russel Ladies.

Gym Club started by Mr Shorten, janitor at Leslie Primary School.
He had been a PT instructor in the army.

West Church Boys' Hockey Team, Christmas day, 1944 taken before
a match with the girls' team.

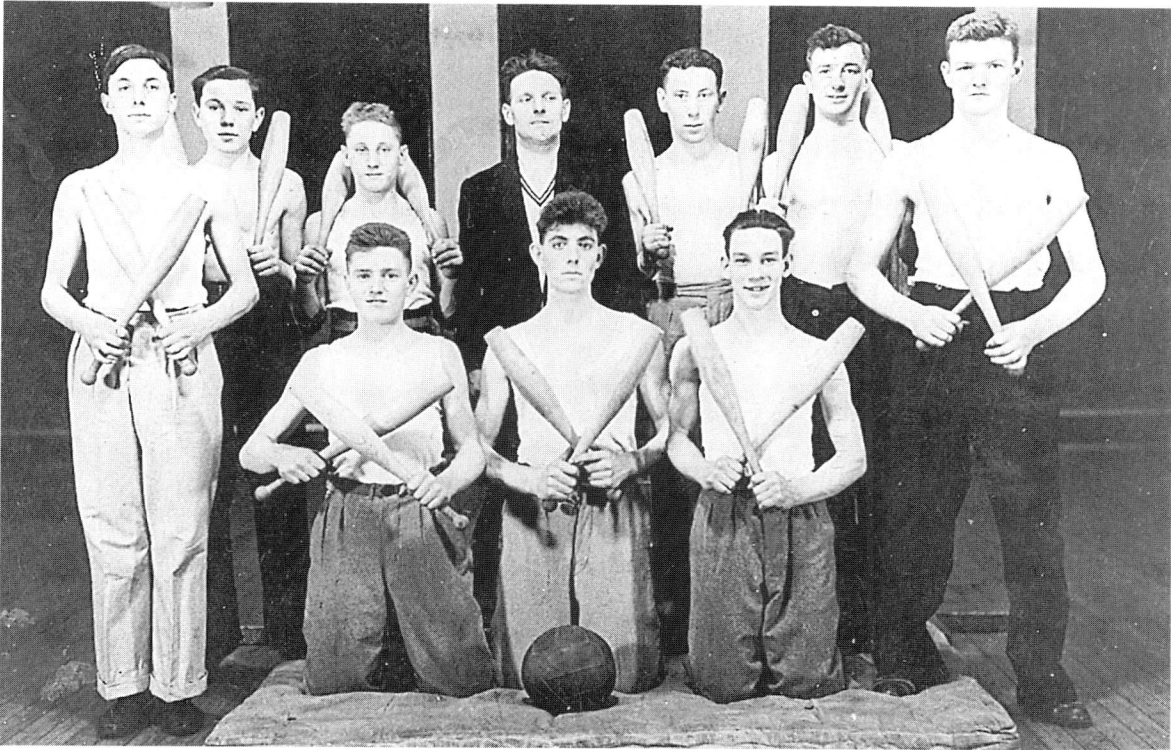

Leslie Gym Club.

Leslie Girl Guides. Captain M. Jobson on the right and Miss C. McGregor on the left.

A. T. C., 1940s.

Leslie Platoon, Black Watch, 1928.

Leslie Platoon, No 4 Coy 6|7 Black Watch, Montrose, 1928.

30

Building of the Leslie viaduct, c1860. The railway opened in 1861.

BOOKS

Buckhaven and Methil in Photographs: £4.95

Robert Brodie: *Historical Sketches of Pathhead and Vicinity* (First published 1863). A facsimile reprint: £5.95

Dysart: £1.00

Jean McKay: *Flutorum: An Investigation into the life of David Hatton 1784 – 1851:* £1.00

Jean McKay: *Wha's Like Us? Characters of Kirkcaldy District:* £1.50

Margaret Nikolic: *Genealogical Microform Holdings in Scottish Libraries:* £6.00

Sheila Campbell: *Family History Sources in Kirkcaldy Central Library:* £2.00

MAPS

Facsimiles

Blaeu map of the Sherifdome of Fife 1654. 1" : 3 miles: £4.20

Victorian Ordnance Survey Map 1" : 1 mile, Sheet 40 Dunfermline & Kirkcaldy: £3.95

Sharp, Greenwood and Fowler, map of the counties of Fife and Kinross, 1828, 1" : 1: mile £8.95

Plan of the town of Kirkcaldy, 1824 by John Wood: £4.95

Street Maps

A selection of local street maps is available including:

Burntisland

Glenrothes

Kirkcaldy

Leven

and surrounding smaller towns: £1.10 – £1.30

POSTCARDS

All postcards: 10p each

Buckhaven, East High Street

Burntisland, High Street, West End

Dysart, St. Serf's Tower and Pan Ha'

Kinghorn Bay

Kirkcaldy, Kirk Wynd

Leven, Bawbee Bridge and Harbour

West Wemyss, Broad Wynd, Church Street

Nicol Ladies, brush sellers